A Gift for You
from Zip.

The Symphony of Australia is the first Musical History of Australia and the first major Work of a brilliant young Australian artist, Gavin Lockley.

A copy of The Symphony of Australia is enclosed for your pleasure, with our Compliments. We hope you enjoy the Book and the Music.

The Symphony of Australia is, like the Zip Hydro-Tap, a Work that Celebrates the Ingenuity of all Australians.

Michael Crouch AO
Executive Chairman

Instant Boiling Water

Symphony of Australia

THE MUSIC   THE STORY

chief conductor & artistic director Gianluigi Gelmetti

Symphony of Australia

THE MUSIC   THE STORY

A new work composed by **Gavin Lockley**

Symphony
of Australia

sydneysymphony

chief conductor & artistic director Gianluigi Gelmetti

First published 2007
Symphony of Australia Pty Ltd
67 Allingham Street
Condell Park NSW 2200

www.symphonyofaustralia.com

National Library of Australia Cataloguing-in-Publication data:

Symphony of Australia: the music, the story: a new work composed by Gavin Lockley.

    ISBN 978 0 980 40800 3 (hbk.).
    1. Symphony of Australia – History. 2. Symphonies – Analysis, appreciation.
    3. Australia – History – Songs and music. I. Lockley, Gavin. II. Symphony of Australia.

784.184

Design and typesetting by Alice Graphics
Project manager Simon Best
Printed in China through Colorcraft Limited, Hong Kong

Contents

Preface

The *Symphony of Australia* is the first major work of a brilliant young Australian composer, Gavin Lockley, a work that celebrates musically what it is to be Australian – our history, our land, our people and the hardships that they suffered, our culture and our spirit.

My wife Shanny and I first heard Gavin Lockley perform on 13 May 1995 at a dinner held to mark the departure of the First Fleet on that day in 1787. A group of school children entertained us, and one of them sang in such a strong, melodious manner that he captured the audience and us in a special way – so much so that it commenced a friendship that we have enjoyed building ever since.

That friendship led to many a discussion on our passions of being Australian. We talked about the need for a piece of music to appeal to the passion and pride of all Australia, and so Gavin conceived *My Country Australia*, which he wrote in May and June 2005. In the course of the year that followed its recording, it was sung by him on Australia Day on national television, at the Bledisloe Cup, and was performed at the Schools Spectacular shown on ABC television. An extraordinary, well deserved reception because it encapsulated the emotion of what it means to be Australian.

It was from this starting point that Gavin composed his Symphony while in England in 2006, perhaps not unlike Australian Dorothea Mackellar who wrote her famous poem 'My Country' – the words that initially inspired Gavin – also while in England, in 1904.

This book has been written to accompany Gavin's music, to remind us of the major events in Australia's history as he perceived them. We hope you too will feel inspired by his music – its world premiere being at the Sydney Opera House in November 2007 – and that it will act as an ambassador to friends overseas and communicate with them that spirit shared by all Australians.

It is that same spirit that is exemplified by Australia's most iconic charity, the Royal Flying Doctor Service of Australia. It is to them and to all Australians that this book is dedicated.

Michael Crouch AO
Sydney
August 2007

The Story

For thousands of years Mother Earth has provided for the people of the land. Through her children she speaks her language of love for all living things on country. Aboriginal people kept this language alive through their lore. Their song, dance and ceremony indicated the importance of caring for country and our spiritual connection to Mother Earth, Australia.

From these ancient beginnings the ships then came and a new Australia was born: a nation of men and women who battled with a harsh and unforgiving environment to build their lives in a new, yet ancient and beautiful world.

This great nation was thus founded on the backs of these pioneers, who suffered extraordinary hardships – hardships that formed the resilient and determined character that we see in the Australian people today.

From a fledgling nation to a nation at war: the sacrifice of the Australian servicemen and women in the defence of our people saw the loss of the flower of generations. A young nation gave its very best to defend its people and its ideals, and the mothers, wives and families bore their unbearable grief for sons that never came home.

From tears of mourning came the joy of rebirth as Australia welcomed the nations of the world to its shores. From Europe to Asia, to the Americas, Africa and the Pacific, the modern Australian nation bloomed in a new and exciting multicultural environment – a world of endless possibilities, excitement and opportunity.

The story of Australia is the story of triumph over adversity, it is the story of a nation of stunning contrasts: drought, flooding rains, beauty and terror. It is the story of a great and proud people with one common goal: to celebrate what we are – our country, our achievements and our exciting future.

The *Symphony of Australia* is the first of its kind. The story about the land and its people unfolds in six movements. The music of the symphony is complemented by this book containing composer's notes, quotations, essays and images of this land, Australia.

Composer's Notes: Movement I *Dreamtime*

Dreamtime – the vision and belief of the Aboriginal people.

At the beginning of time there is a violent sequence of cataclysms. The world remains unformed and the earth roars. Then there is emptiness with no life, only silence and nothingness. The land is still.

The Rainbow Serpent awakes. The world through the serpent slowly comes to life, culminating in the serpent's search for its home tribe, which takes it on a fantastic journey across the continent, forming valleys and mountains, rivers and deserts with its massive form. The journey becomes frenetic as it nears the top country and Cape York.

The Rainbow Serpent listens and hears the 'Voices of the Cape': the heartbeat of the land, a new dawn and the elements around it. The first form of the 'Australia' theme is heard. We then hear the sounds of the land, the beauty of the water, the magic of wind in the trees and the sound of fire.

The Rainbow Serpent's time of peace passes. Not recognising the northern voices, it searches for its home tribe, which it finally finds at the meeting of two rivers. Two brothers (represented by flute and oboe) try to camp inside the Serpent's mouth, which they mistake for a cave. The Rainbow Serpent unwittingly swallows them.

The Rainbow Serpent then flees with the tribe in pursuit. The tribe cuts open the Serpent and the brothers emerge as lorikeets. The Rainbow Serpent's spirit becomes the rainbow itself.

Lake Argyle, Northern Territory

Dreamtime

It was one thing to persuade a surveyor that a heap of boulders were the eggs of the Rainbow Snake, or a lump of reddish sandstone was the liver of a speared kangaroo. It was something else to convince him that a featureless stretch of gravel was the musical equivalent of Beethoven's Opus III.

From *The Songlines* by Bruce Chatwin

Rainbow Serpent, Mount Borradaile, Arnhem Land, Northern Territory. Aboriginal paintings, dated as far back as 50,000 years old, provide a visual record of the spiritual beliefs and historical events that are the heritage of the world's oldest surviving culture.

S ome eighty million years before the emergence of humankind, Australia was part of Gondwana, a southern super-continent that included present-day New Guinea, New Zealand, Antarctica, India, and parts of Africa and South America. Over millions and millions of years Gondwana had slowly broken up into subcontinents and these great masses of land gradually drifted apart to where they are positioned today. It is believed that the first people to come to Australia did so by sea, and their crossing could only have occurred during the Pleistocene period – or Ice Age – when sea levels were significantly lower than they are today. These immigrants probably crossed the waters between the numerous islands of Sundaland, the extension of southeast Asia, which included Indonesia. They then had to have undertaken a longer sea voyage to Sahul, which was the subcontinent made up of Tasmania, mainland Australia and New Guinea.

When the ice began to melt and sea levels steadily rose, enormous areas became submerged and many of the islands of Sundaland – which once acted like stepping-stones – disappeared. Australia was separated from New Guinea, and Tasmania cut off from the mainland. It has been estimated that during this time Australia's original inhabitants numbered approximately 300,000; and when it became an island continent, they too were effectively severed from the rest of the world. Not only did migration to these shores cease, but also for thousands of years Australia was insulated from further immigration. The Aboriginal people were thus impervious to the influences, developments, customs, ideas or beliefs of any other civilisation beyond their shores. That the ancient civilisation of Rome lasted twelve centuries is impressive. But it is astounding to discover that until the British settlement in 1788 Australia's original inhabitants had lived in the oldest continuous civilisation in the world dating back at least 50,000 years.

In 1606 a young Dutchman named Willem Janz sailed over uncharted seas and came upon the unexplored coast of Australia's Cape York. He later wrote that 'there was no good to be done there', and described the inhabitants to be 'wild, cruel, black savages'. Eighty years later, the English buccaneer William Dampier, said much the same, that the Aborigines were 'the miserablest people in the world', and 'setting aside their human shape, they differ but little from brutes'. Then, almost a century after Dampier, Captain James Cook presented a significantly different view when he happened upon the eastern coast of Australia. There he found a people not at all like those described by Janz and Dampier. Cook wrote:

'... they may appear to some to be the most wretched People upon Earth; but in reality they are far more happier than we Europeans, being wholly unacquainted not only with the Superfluous, but with the necessary Conveniences so much sought after in Europe; they are happy in not knowing the use of them. They live in a Tranquility which is not disturbed by the Inequality of Condition. The earth and Sea of their own accord furnishes them with all things necessary for Life. They covet not Magnificient Houses, Household-stuff, etc.; they live in a Warm and fine Climate, and enjoy every wholesome Air, so that they have very little need of Cloathing; and this they seem to be fully sencible of, for many to whom we gave Cloth, etc., left it carelessly upon the Sea beach and in the Woods, as a thing they had no manner of use for.'

Although Cook paints an idyllic picture, like Janz and Dampier, he could not look beyond surface appearances, and that is because the Aboriginal way of life did not in any way relate to the European concept of progress.

Centuries before white man discovered Australia, he had begun to fashion a distinct and perhaps inflated image of himself as a master of nature. By the early seventeenth century, when Willem Janz had set sail on his voyage to New Guinea, all of Europe was evidence of the great advances the white man had made in trade, science and technology. These advances moulded him to view the world in terms of discovery and conquest for material wealth. Not only did technology allow him to master nature to fit his present interests, it made him feel that he had risen above nature.

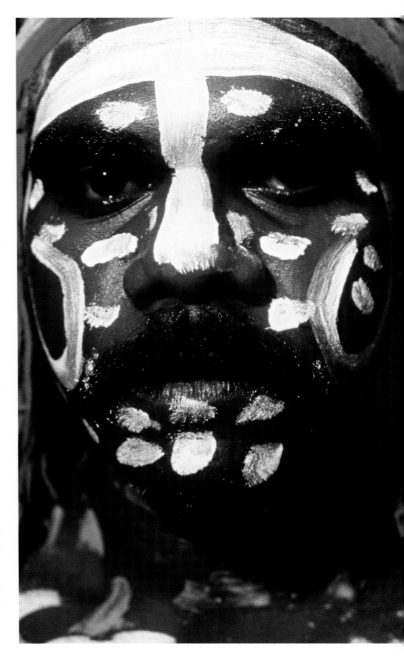

Walpa Gorge at Kata Tjuta ('many heads' in the local Pitjantjatjara language), also known as The Olgas. The rock formation is made up of rounded domes that have been shaped by the elements over millions of years.

Aboriginal elder from the Pintubi tribe, Northern Territory.

So much so that when the European explorers arrived, their assumption was that Australia's Indigenous people were akin to prehistoric man. What they saw were hunter–gatherers whose tools had 'progressed' no further than the use of stone, wood or bone to hunt and prepare their food. Nor had these people mastered any form of agriculture or the domestication of animals.

It was a mistaken assumption. The European mind was incapable of conceiving that something more complex than the singular need for food could guide and structure the Indigenous way of life. What of their paintings, songs, dances, and stories? Certainly this was rich evidence that the Aboriginal was not the purposeless or deperson-

alised human being that the accounts of Janz, Dampier, Cook and others would have lead people to believe. The white man simply could not imagine that their mysterious creative activities could be as important, if not more important, than the few tools the Indigenous people had developed to aid their survival. With the blinkers of 'progress' the European probably thought of Aboriginal ritual culture as mere mumbo-jumbo. How could sacred Aboriginal rock paintings, for example, be compared to towering edifices of Christian faith such as Notre Dame in Paris, the Basilica of St John Lateran in Rome, or Westminster Cathedral in London?

Despite his visible 'advantage', the white man could not fathom that the ritual symbolic prac-

tices of Aboriginal people were – and to this day continue to be – manifestations of their belief in the Dreamtime, which is the essence of their culture and of their very being. The Dreamtime, or the Dreaming as it is sometimes called, is a complex and advanced form of thinking that incorporates religious belief, social mores, cultural identity, and knowledge of natural phenomena. To comprehend the Dreamtime one has to be initiated into the paradoxical space of a 'time before time' when the world was void and formless, and ancestral spirits or deities emerged from within the earth and brought the world into existence.

These totemic spirits appeared in both animal and human form and went on long journeys to

Garaabara, a word from the Dharug Aborginal language heard by the first Europeans at Port Jackson became today's word corroboree, meaning an assembly of sacred, festive or warlike character.

create the trees, mountains, rivers, lakes, plants, all the animals, wind, sky, sun, moon, and everything else. Their journeys were recorded in Dreaming tracks or Songlines, which are invisible pathways formed by the landmarks where totemic spirits were known to have passed by or had come to rest. These landmarks are identified as sacred sites.

The Dreamtime has many different meanings; perhaps as many meanings as there are Aboriginal clans. What this means is that there are innumerable localised Dreamings or Songlines that were sung by ancestral beings who took on widely differing forms and personalities. For example, one particular clan might say they have a Kangaroo Dreaming, while another might have a Wallaby Dreaming; yet another will have a Lizard Dreaming, or a Frog Dreaming, or, apparently, even a Virus Dreaming. Each totemic ancestor had fashioned itself from the formless earth and then fashioned the country to which the clan would belong. Each Dreaming is therefore a different version of the universal song of creation.

Indigenous art takes many forms: ancient engravings and rock art, designs in sand or on the body, exquisite fibre craft and wooden sculptures, bark paintings and more recently an explosion of brilliant contemporary painting.

The function of Dreamtime stories is to teach or remind one to look beyond the limited horizons of the self. They exemplify the intimate link between the people and the country. An Aboriginal person does not look upon themselves as a separate and independent being in the world, but a being of the world. Where a non-Aboriginal person might declare, 'I own this land', an Aboriginal person will say, 'I am this land.' That their ancestors could and would migrate from one form to another – as, say, from human to rock or animal to water – is illustrative of their belief in the fundamental interconnectedness of the universe.

The phrase 'time before time' marvellously suggests that the Dreamtime is not something to be found in 'long-ago', but in the always 'here and now'. It is a living force – all that was and all that ever will be is. Each and every ceremonial re-enactment or retelling of a Dreamtime episode is more than a dramatic explanation of the origins of natural phenomena, it is the re-creation of the Creation.

And so we come to understand the Dreamtime, as inherited by the oldest civilisation in the world.

*Three views of First Fleet store ship **Borrowdale** (Francis Holman c. 1787). Commanded by Captain Readthorn Hobson, the ship was only 75 feet long with a beam of 22 feet.*

Composer's Notes: Movement II *The Ships*

The arrival of the First Fleet that departed from England on 13 May 1787.

A convict reflects on the home he has left behind and the harrowing voyage to Botany Bay on the First Fleet. Drums represent the violence and thrill of a high seas adventure. A piccolo folk tune is developed and then engulfed by the 'theme of the sea'. Strummed strings depict the rigging of the ship and the activity onboard. The canon of the folk song represents the great throng of convicts, a mass of humanity kept in appalling conditions. The pace quickens as the roaring forties winds propel the ships to their destination.

The fleet arrives, described by the sound world of 1788 at Port Jackson. Sound elements are juxtaposed to represent the original Aboriginal inhabitants being overwhelmed by the invaders and the ships' companies marching to fife and drum to hear the first sermon based on Psalm 116: 12 'What shall I render unto the Lord for all his benefits toward me'.

The sermon thanks God for his blessings and speaks of giving back to God in return for all the benefits we have received. The founding of a great nation is acknowledged. The movement draws to a close with the previously overwhelmed voices of the original inhabitants echoing down the ages, asserting their place as the original and rightful protectors and inhabitants of the land.

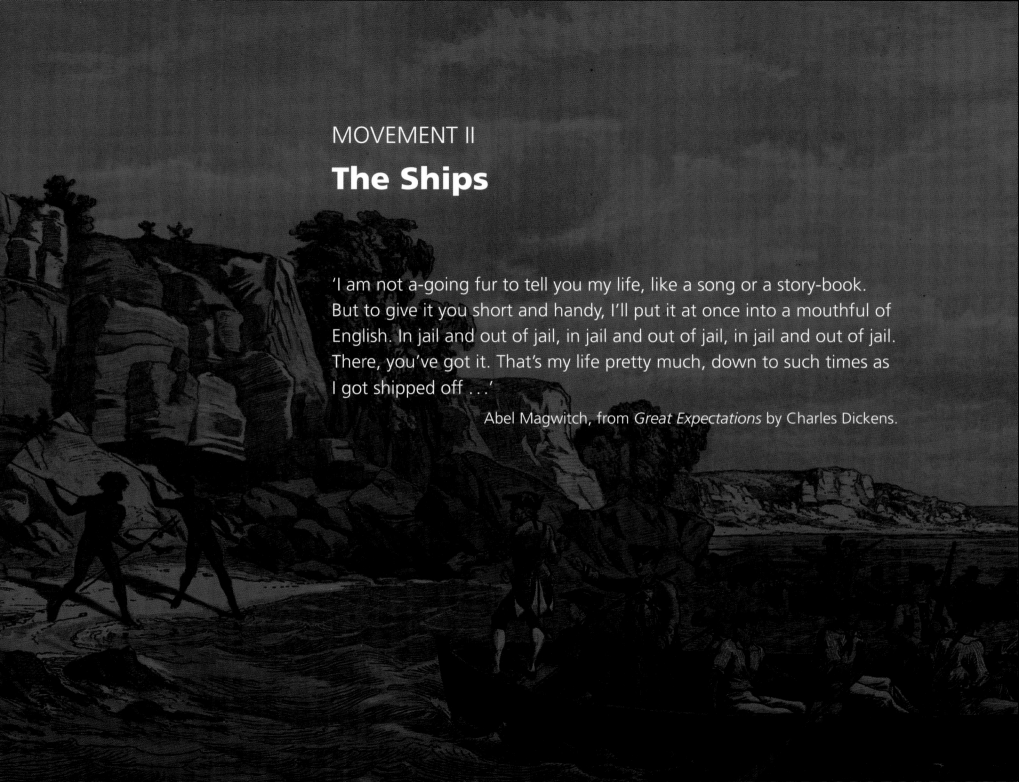

MOVEMENT II

The Ships

'I am not a-going fur to tell you my life, like a song or a story-book.
But to give it you short and handy, I'll put it at once into a mouthful of
English. In jail and out of jail, in jail and out of jail, in jail and out of jail.
There, you've got it. That's my life pretty much, down to such times as
I got shipped off ...'

Abel Magwitch, from *Great Expectations* by Charles Dickens.

Captain Cook's landing at Botany, A.D. 1770. This is a nineteenth-century artist's impression of Cook's first encounter with Australian Aborigines. The lithograph was provided free with a Christmas edition of the Sydney **Town and Country** *journal, 21 December, 1872.*

The novel *Great Expectations* is a brilliant work of fiction, yet the place where the convict Magwitch 'got shipped off' to was a historical reality. It was the penal settlement of New South Wales, which was as real to the people of eighteenth-century England as the world today is to us.

In 1770, ninety years before Charles Dickens had written *Great Expectations*, Captain James Cook planted England's flag on the shores of Botany Bay. That was the first significant event in Australia's colonial history. Another significant event came seventeen years later when the First Fleet, under the command of Captain Arthur Phillip, set sail from Portsmouth on 13 May 1787, bound for Botany Bay.

But it seemed no-one in England could imagine this event as the beginning of a great new nation. An unknown reporter for the *London Chronicle* wrote the following news item: 'This afternoon passed by the Ram-head, through the Sound, the men of war, store-ships, etc., under command of Commodore Philips [sic], for Botany Bay; and the wind was fair, and blows strong, they must soon be out of the Channel.' Written with such indifference, it is difficult to believe this item actually reports the departure of the First Fleet. Moreover the news item appeared on 27 May, seven days after the whole fleet had left.

No doubt it was the wretched human cargo (note the use of 'etc.') aboard the First Fleet that influenced the tenor of the *Chronicle*'s report that day. Apart from the two 'men-of-war' – armed naval vessels – and three store-ships, included in the Fleet were six transports carrying 789 convict men, women and children. In the opinion of the day, a cargo of felons could hardly have been considered worthy stock with which to build a nation. It has been said that on 13 May the shutters of shops went up for the first time since January, when the convict ships were at Portsmouth in preparation for the long journey.

The transportation of convicts to southern colonies was not something newly introduced by the then British penal system. England had regularly shipped convicts to America during the eighteenth century. But in 1782 that program was disrupted when England was defeated in the American War of Independence. By 12 October 1786, when the British government authorised the establishment of the colony of New South Wales, there was something more urgent on the government's agenda than the inauguration of a nation.

So, for the majority of Britons the transportation of convicts to Botany Bay was the solution to their miserably overcrowded jails. Between January 1788, when the First Fleet arrived at Botany Bay, and November 1823, over 37,000 felons were

Captain Cook taking possession of the Australian continent on behalf of the British Crown, 1770, under the name of New South Wales. Drawn and engraved by Samuel Calvert (1828–1913) from the great historical painting by Gilfillan in the possession of the Royal Society of Victoria.

Prison hulk loading, by Samuel Atkins (1787–1808).

landed at the new colony of New South Wales. Thousands more followed until 1867 when the last convict ship arrived at Australia shores.

On 13 May 1787, what would the convicts have felt as they heard the signal to weigh anchor? Were they deeply saddened when they sensed the ships slowly pulling away from the coast of England? Did some feel a hurtful wound knowing they were not welcome in their homeland? Did others just tremble in fear at the thought of a long and arduous journey with greater hardship at the other end? Or shiver with hope at the prospect of a new future in a faraway land?

In *A Narrative of the Expedition to Botany Bay*, Watkin Tench, a captain of the First Fleet marines, wrote: 'By ten o'clock we had got clear of the Isle of Wight, at which time, having very little pleasure in conversing with my own thoughts, I strolled down among the convicts to observe their sentiments at this juncture. A very few excepted, their countenances indicated a high degree of satisfaction, though in some the pang of being severed, perhaps forever, from their native land could not be wholly suppressed.'

The convicts were on their way to one of the remotest corners of the earth, a place untamed and completely unfamiliar, and the best they could expect once they got there were several years of forced labour. Yet, according to Tench's account, the reactions of the majority were markedly good-humoured. Indeed, to the point that one might envisage the more adventuresome convicts gathered together and, with the aid of a little rum, having a good sing-a-long.

Farewell to olde England forever
Farewell to my olde pals as well
Farewell to the well-known Old Bailey
Where I once used to look such a swell
Singing too-ral li-ooral li-ad-dity
Singing too-ral li-ooral li-ay

For those convicts who had been condemned to death the occasion was obviously thought to be heaven sent. They would have expressed great relief, and with their spirits buoyed they may even have entertained thoughts of a tide of good fortune still to come, particularly those sentenced for trivial crimes.

Mary Founes, a servant woman forty-three years old, must surely have thanked providence. In 1784 she was sentenced to death for highway robbery. Like many others in her position, Founes was saved from the gallows on condition she serve a seven-year sentence at Botany Bay. Even if she had not been condemned to death, Botany Bay seemed to be a considerably better option than serving her sentence in England. She had no trade skills, and with her reputation as a servant woman vastly diminished, she would have been forced into crime again or else end up in squalor.

As she was led aboard the *Lady Penrhyn*, Mary Founes knew life would be hard for the next

The Founding of Australia. By Capt. Arthur Phillip R.N. Sydney Cove, Jan. 26th 1788,
(Algernon Talmage, 1871–1939).

A depiction of the convict rebellion at Castle Hill, also known as the Battle of Vinegar Hill, one of the first significant conflicts in Australia's early colonial history. The picture's inscription reads: 'Major Johnston with Quartermaster Laycock and twenty five privates of ye New South Wales Corps defeats two hundred and sixty six armed rebels, 5th March 1804.'

seven years, but she also thought about the life she might be able to have at the end of those years. Freedom and wellbeing, and the chance of an honest and decent life untaxed by poverty.

Before the First Fleet had sailed, very little thought was given to assessing the health of each convict and selecting those who looked best suited to withstand a long sea voyage. It was a difficult voyage for the convicts. For a time, at least until the ships were on the open sea, leg irons restricted their movements. When unshackled, convicts were warned in no uncertain terms that transgressions would be dealt with swiftly and harshly. Even at the slightest show of disobedience or impertinence an officer would not hesitate to call for the 'cat of nine tails' to quell a convict's rebellious spirit.

Between the decks, where the convicts were housed, the air did not circulate freely and quickly turned foul. Not having experienced sea voyages before, many of the convicts suffered from sea-sickness, which added to the stench. Fevers were prevalent. Sores from splinters or leg irons were easily infected by the filth, while their bedding was rarely taken above deck to air, or allowed to dry if wet.

There was no such thing as a balanced diet, and having to go several months without fresh supplies of food, particularly vegetables, meant that scurvy was a constant threat. Dysentery was a further curse, and if a convict fell ill to a mysterious disease, this unfortunate person was likely to be bled several times by the ship's surgeon.

The rigours of the voyage were far worse on the women convicts. They suffered the same harrowing conditions as the men, yet were provided with far less food to sustain them on the long voyage. The reason behind such a strange ordinance was a simple one: the men had to be kept as fit as possible for the inevitable work to be done once the Fleet arrived at Botany Bay.

Punishment for breach of rules was just as severe on the women convicts as on the men. When officers on the *Lady Penrhyn* abandoned flogging 'on the naked breech', they did so only because such punishment could not be inflicted without proper 'attention to decency'. But, with respect to decency, the officers demonstrated their resourcefulness. They resorted to a few other effective disciplinary methods, including the use of thumbscrews, cutting off the women's hair and shaving their heads, or gagging and binding them for days at a time. Pleas of compassion were likely to be rejected, or exploited to gain sexual favours.

Captain Watkin Tench noted that by the time the First Fleet had laid anchor at Botany Bay only twenty-three convicts had died. He implores the reader to consider what a surprising achievement this was. In fact the reader's surprise should 'redouble' for, as Tench wrote, '... it must be remembered that the people thus sent out were not a ship's company starting with every advantage of health and good living, which a state of freedom produces; but the major part a miserable set of convicts, emaciated from confinement, and in want of cloaths and almost every convenience to render so long a passage tolerable.' Tench could not have known what was in store.

When Mary Founes was taken aboard the Lady Penrhyn, she may have counted her blessings too soon. No, Mary didn't die at sea. But her seven-year sentence was unintentionally commuted to six months. She died at Sydney Cove on 25 June 1788. The harsh conditions of her voyage and those at the colony were undeniably the main reasons for her death. Perhaps her original sentence would have been a blessing after all.

Others fared worse. Rebecca Boulton died on 4 March 1788, not two months since disembarking at Sydney Cove, and she was not even a convict. She was a child who sailed with her convicted mother on the *Prince of Wales*. Her mother, also named Rebecca, died a month later. Perhaps she died from heartbreak.

Little thought was given to the state of health of the convicts before leaving Portsmouth. Later at Sydney Cove it became evident that the architects of the penal colony had not had the foresight to consider the types or people required to establish it. When the First Fleet had arrived at Sydney Cove on 26 January 1788, only two among the throng of convicts were farmers, a few others had carpentry or brick-making skills, while the majority were said to be thieves and prostitutes with an aversion to labour.

Six months after the landing only 200 out of the 750 or so surviving convicts were working at clearing land and building storehouses. All of the others were either under medical treatment for scurvy and other ailments, considered too old or unfit to work, or were just plain vagabonds. The colony's food supply was ill-nourishing and rapidly diminishing. Shelter was inadequate, sometimes primitive. Twenty-three convicts died in the course of a nine-month sea voyage, but in the six months after landing twenty-eight convicts and seven children had died.

Six months earlier most of the convicts, both men and women, may have thought their woes had come to an end when they came ashore at Sydney Cove in Port Jackson. But they had just begun.

So too had the nation.

MOVEMENT III *The Red Centre*

The exploration of Australia – depicted by the Burke and Wills expedition.

The expedition led by Burke and Wills (represented by timpanists) crosses the continent in an unforgiving environment. The Red Centre overwhelms them in recurring waves of sound, each representing the merciless rising of the Australian sun. As nature increases its force, the greater the explorers' determination becomes. The pace quickens as they strive to reach their goal: the Gulf of Carpentaria.

Overwhelmed by the heat as it distorts their perception of the horizon, the explorers confront the reality of failure, and their own mortality. Flies, rodents, rocks and mud are some of the elements they have to struggle against. When their goal is near there is one further ascent of the sun and they try to make it to the gulf with all the energy they possess. The 'Australia' theme recurs as they anticipate the success of their journey. However, at the point of triumph they are defeated by the mangrove swamps from reaching the ocean. Burke's despair and thoughts of home and his beloved Julia Mathews are depicted in a poignant version of the 'Australia' theme on solo piano.

As they make their way back south, the relentless sun makes each day hell. The Red Centre finally takes their lives as they tragically miss the rescue party by six hours within one single, solitary day.

MOVEMENT III
The Red Centre

Out on the wastes of the Never-Never,
That's where the dead men lie,
There where the heat-wave dances forever,
That's where the dead men lie …

From *Where the Dead Men Lie* by Barcroft Boake

Gulf of
Carpentaria

Outbound route ●●●●●
Return route (approx.) ●●●●●

0   200   400 kilometres

Flinders River
Cloncurry River
Corella Creek

Selwyn Ranges

Burke River

Kings Creek

Diamantina River

Sturts Stony Creek

Cooper's Creek

Bulloo River

Torowotto Swamp

Menindee

Balranald

Swan Hill

Melbourne

The unknown has always tempted the imagination. From the arrival of the First Fleet in 1788 the conquest of Australia's interior lured the hearts of visionary men and fired their minds with dreams of glory.

But it was necessity that first and foremost stoked those fires.

Commodore Arthur Phillip looked for arable land near an abundant source of fresh water. He was well aware that without such necessities the new colony would not survive. By the time he resigned as governor in 1792, the new settlement had made very little expansion into Australia's interior. The only image of the colony's progress that he could take back to England was of a patch of Parramatta under cultivation. But Phillip was acutely aware of point where dream and necessity meet, for that small corner of Parramatta was emblematic of the future he had envisioned for the colony. He had set the infant colony on a course of inland exploration for self-reliance. In the years to come, as more ships arrived and the population grew, the need for fresh water, good soil and grazing land played an enormous part in further explorations of Australia's interior.

So too did the curiosity and personal ambitions of the explorers. Captain Watkin Tench wrote: 'To an active and contemplative mind a new country is an inexhaustible source of curiosity and speculation.' What was the continent like at its heart?

Was there truth to the rumour circulating among the convicts of an Eden beyond the mountains, or of an escape route to China? And why did so many of the great rivers flow west? Was there a vast inland sea?

Many set off by both sea and land to find the answers. Hundreds of brave and enduring pioneers, many of whose names are not recorded, helped reveal the secrets of a land mass shown on early world maps with its interior as a blank space. Those whose names have become legends include Bass and Flinders who circumnavigated the continent and Sturt who was first to explore the inland rivers. Inland pioneers whose names are part of Australia's history and commemorated in names of places, highways and rivers include Eyre, Grey, Hovell, Hume, Leichhardt, Mitchell and Stuart: The Red Centre, once referred to as the 'Never Never', now has a lot more on the map, and is important for mining, agriculture and tourism.

Some of the pioneers who ventured into the unknown came back triumphant. Others were forced to return home with their spirits tapered, beaten back by either an unforgiving land or the hard fact that their dream was indeed as tangible as a mirage. Some, though making important discoveries , never returned.

In 1860 Robert O'Hara Burke, a dashing police superintendent, headed an expedition like no other. It was the most expensive to date, better equipped than any previous expedition, and it was the most audacious. The goal was to traverse the continent from Melbourne in the south to the Gulf of Carpentaria in the north.

On 20 August 1860 the expedition set out from Melbourne's Royal Park. In Burke's words, 'No expedition has ever started under such favourable circumstances as this.' But that was far from the truth. Burke had no experience as an explorer, and historians have suggested that he enthusiastically petitioned for command of the expedition in order to win the hand of Julia Mathews, a theatre star fifteen years his junior.

Despite the electricity in the air brought on by a crowd of 15,000 well-wishers, the expedition's progress even on the first day was not encouraging. When the expedition made first camp for the night, it had travelled not much more than ten kilometres, an unimpressive achievement, especially in the eyes of an irascible man like Burke.

When dream overtakes necessity the consequences can be disastrous. Burke's dream tugged at his heart and weighed on his mind. On that first night, he abandoned camp and galloped back to Melbourne to propose to Julia Mathews. She promised to give him an answer upon his return from the north. When Burke arrived back at camp the next morning, around his neck was a pouch containing a lock of Julia's hair.

Memorandum of the Start of the Exploring Expedition, 1860
(Nicholas Chevalier, 1828–1902, Melbourne, oil on canvas)

Burke, Wills and King at Cooper's Creek (Photograph by Alfred Abbott, 1838–72, from Waxworks Museum, Melbourne)

The expedition reached Swan Hill in three weeks and one of the troubles along the way was a threat to arrest Burke over the matter of a dishonoured cheque. Burke ardently spurred his men on, even though his planned route was hazy at best. Torrential rains slowed their progress, and as they crossed the Murray River, it dawned on Burke that they were overburdened by the amount of equipment and supplies. When they arrived at Balranald on 14 September the morale of the men was low, particularly the wagon drivers, and so Burke decided to lighten the load by selling off things he considered useless. However, some items were quite essential, such as the supply of lime juice to prevent scurvy.

Then tensions flared at Menindee between Burke and his deputy, George Landells, over the care of the camels. The wagons made little progress over rough terrain, so Burke wanted to transfer some of the load onto the camels. Landells insisted the camels should be kept strong for their inevitable march across desert areas. Landells resigned and returned to Melbourne. To replace Landells as second-in-command, Burke appointed a brilliant young surveyor by the name of William John Wills. He also employed William Wright, a local of Menindee who had worked as a station manager, to direct the expedition to Cooper's Creek.

Burke was poisoned by impatience. He discharged some of the men, shed more of the cargo, particularly the scientific equipment, and decided on a plan to split the expedition in two. First, Wright was to guide an advance party to Torowoto swamp from which the party would advance to establish a depot at Cooper's Creek. Second, Wright would then return to Menindee from Torowoto and immediately bring up the second party with the bulk of provisions.

The advance party waited for weeks at Cooper's Creek and still there was no sign of Wright who was returning from Mendindee as planned. Burke could not bear any further delay. With characteristic folly he threw caution to the wind and resolved to make a dash for the Gulf with three of his most loyal men – Wills, John King and Charlie Gray. Burke placed William Brahe in command of the depot with instructions to wait three months for Burke's return, but Wills requested Brahe linger another month.

Burke handed to Brahe a mysterious parcel of sealed papers. If the parcel contained intimate letters to Julia Mathews, we will never know. Brahe was entrusted to destroy the parcel if Burke failed to return.

Historians have speculated over what the four men expected to experience when they finally reached their destination. The reality of the gruelling terrain as they neared the Gulf would quickly have driven away any fanciful thoughts. It was the monsoon season and constant rain turned the ground into thick black syrup, bogging the

Return of Burke and Wills to Cooper's Creek, 1868 (Nicholas Chevalier, 1828–1902)

The Burke and Wills 'Dig Tree' is one of Australia's national icons and an enduring reminder of the pioneering spirit and extreme harshness of the outback. (Frank Clune 1893–1971)

camels. Burke ordered King and Gray to stay behind near the coast and look after the camels while he and Wills strived to reach the ocean.

On 9 February 1861 Burke and Wills stumbled across a stream that had water too salty to drink and showed the rise and fall of ocean tides. Knowing the sea was near, their march forward was irrepressible. By 11 February the pair had managed to push ahead at least another 20 kilometres only to be confronted by an impenetrable mangrove swamp. They fell to their knees exhausted, and felt utter dejection. Usually diligent in keeping his diary up-to-date, Wills did not bother with an entry for that day. Burke would write later: 'It would be well to say that we reached the sea, but

we could not obtain a view of the open ocean although we made every endeavour to do so.' To have come so far and be barred from the sea by a few kilometres was painful, unbearably so.

But worse was yet to come. Burke, Wills, King and Gray now had to trek 1,500 kilometres back to Cooper's Creek with reduced supplies and less time to complete the arduous journey. Nine weeks into the return journey Gray had begun to complain that he was growing weaker by the minute. Not only could he hardly walk, his words were gibberish nonsense. His companions thought he was feigning weakness to secure a greater share of the rations. When Gray died soon after, their sense of guilt compelled them to stop and bury him. Under the burning sun it took the trio a whole day to dig the grave.

By 20 April Burke, Wills and King knew Cooper's Creek was close by, perhaps 50 or 60 kilometres away. The next morning they mustered whatever strength they had left and stubbornly put one foot in front of the other. They staggered on through what felt like a furnace, and just as the sun began to set Burke was certain he could see the camp. The trio were in despair when they marched into camp and found it was deserted. Why?

It was Wills who noticed a tree with the message 'DIG 3FT NW APR 21 1861' hacked into it. The date looked promising, perhaps they had just set off or moved camp further along the creek.

They dug up a cache and amid a small supply of food was a letter. It said that Brahe had had troubles of his own. Wright had not arrived with the rest of the stores, and one of his men was seriously injured and needed attention. After having waited more than four months Brahe decided to return to Menindee that morning. Burke, Wills and King slumped down in disbelief. They had missed Brahe's departure by a day. Had they not stopped to bury Gray they would have been on their way home. That evening Burke, Wills and King may well have wondered why fate had dealt them such a cruel hand.

Against the better judgement of Wills and King, rather than pursue Brahe, Burke insisted they head south-west to Mount Hopeless, where there stood a sheep station. He reasoned that Brahe had fresh horses and camels and they would never catch up. Besides, Menindee was 600 kilometres away while Mount Hopeless was only 150, and they could follow Cooper's Creek, which flowed in that direction.

But again they were to experience bitter disappointment. The creek ran dry in the sand and ahead of them was open desert. They made one attempt to dash across the desert, but after only a few kilometres the unbearable heat and their thirst forced them to retreat to Cooper's Creek. There they survived for several weeks but only due to the kindness of an Aboriginal clan that appeared to live along the creek. Then one morning the Aborigines had disappeared and Burke, Wills and King were left to fend for themselves.

On 26 June Wills collapsed exhausted and malnourished, and could not move. He knew he was no longer capable of clinging to life and suggested Burke and King set off in search of the Aborigines, otherwise they had little chance of survival. On that day Wills composed a letter to his father that began, 'These are probably the last lines you will ever get from me.' He died on or about the 29 June 1861.

On the first day of their search Burke and King had not gone far when Burke began to complain of great pains in his legs and back. By the end the third day Burke's legs had given up and he was convinced 'he could not last many hours.' He handed King his watch and pocketbook and requested that King stay by his side until he was 'quite dead'.

Then Burke went quiet. As he lay dying, all of his actions over the past eleven months were now a matter between him and his conscience. With little time left he wrote his last letter. However, it was not to Julia Mathews, but his sister Hessie, revoking a will he had made to Julia in an instance of amorous impetuosity. In the face of death Burke kept his calm, reviewed his actions and found them wanting. The dream was over.

On 2 November 1861 Melbourne received the news that King was found alive but that Burke and Wills were dead. Ever since, the enterprise has

been written into history as the Burke and Wills expedition. When the news broke, Julia Mathews was appearing at the Princess Theatre and she still had Burke's locket dangling from around her neck. The next day, she was walking through the botanical gardens, her neck bare.

Flying foxes fill the sky above Norman River, Gulf of Carpentaria, Queensland.

Composer's notes: MOVEMENT IV *Pie Jesu*

A lament for all Australians who have been sacrificed in wars.

A mother receives a letter informing her of her son's death on the battlefield in World War I. She prays for strength, singing the words '*Pie Jesu, qui tollis peccata mundi, Agnus Dei qui tollis peccata mundi, dona eis requiem*' (Blessed Jesus, who takes away the sins of the world, Lamb of God who takes away the sins of the world, give us rest).

The sacred lyrics of the 'Pie Jesu' highlight the significance of sacrifice, in particular of those Australians who died for their country in the two world wars. They laid down their lives so that others may live. In this way the Australian servicemen and women can be seen to be Christ-like.

The focal point of the movement lies in that moment of extreme grief that so many mothers, family and friends experience upon learning that their loved ones will never return home: a simple message has changed their lives forever.

A view from a lifeboat carrying Australians of the 1st Divisional Signal Company as they are towed towards Anzac Cove at 6 a.m. on the day of the Gallipoli landing, 25 April 1915.

MOVEMENT IV
Pie Jesu

With proud thanksgiving, a mother for her children,
England mourns for her dead across the sea.
Flesh of her flesh they were, spirit of spirit,
Fallen in the cause of the free.

…

They shall grow not old, as we that are left grow old:
Age shall not weary them, nor the years condemn.
At the going down of the sun and in the morning
We will remember them.

Extract from *For the Fallen* by Laurence Binyon (1869–1943)

*Mrs Lindorff (left), a mother of four members of
the Australian imperial Force (two of whom died of
wounds during service), and friend, paying her respects
during the Anzac Day commemoration ceremony in
Melbourne. (Printed in* Herald Sun, *24 April 1943)*

Issued by the N.S.W RECRUITING COMMITTEE.   JOHN SANDS Ltd

WIN THE WAR LEAGUE
I SERVE

FOLLOW YOUR MATES
ENLIST.

Posters encouraged young Australian men to sign up and do their duty for their nation. Thousands of young Australian men lied about their age in order to qualify for enlistment in the armed forces in both world wars.

The fuse that triggered the explosion of World War I across Europe was an eighteen-year-old Bosnian student who seized an unexpected opportunity to fire off two gunshots that killed the heir to the Austro-Hungarian throne, Archduke Franz Ferdinand, and his wife Sophia, on 28 June 1914 in Sarajevo, the capital of Bosnia. Austria was outraged, as were other European nations. Although Bosnia (as well as Herzegovina) was a province under Austro-Hungarian administration, the assassination provided Austria with an excuse to mobilise against Serbia. It was no secret that Serbia felt the provinces of Bosnia and Herzegovina should belong to a pan-Slavic state led by Serbia. On 23 July, and confident of Germany's support, Austria declared war on neighbouring Serbia convinced that Serbia was responsible.

How did such a distant event, so far removed from the everyday concerns of a people on the other side of the globe, propel Australia into one of the most lethal conflicts of the twentieth century?

An ominous chain of events ensued: Russia intervened in defence of Serbia, which compelled Germany to mobilise its army against both Russia and its ally France. Then in an effort to gain military advantage over France, Germany attempted to overrun Belgium. While Britain had earlier taken steps to contain the tensions, as guarantor of Belgian neutrality, on 4 August it had no other choice but to go to war with Germany.

Australia – as did New Zealand and Canada – looked beyond the fact that this was a European war and rallied behind the mother country. Even before the fighting had begun, Australia had made moves to come to Britain's aid. The words of Prime Minister Joseph Cook left no doubt whatsoever about Australia's position: 'When the Empire is at war, Australia is at war.'

Equally keen to commit Australia to the British cause was Andrew Fisher, the Leader of the Labor Party. He proclaimed, 'Should the worst happen after everything has been done that honour will permit, we Australians will help defend the mother country to our last man and our last shilling.' Within six weeks of the declaration of war Fisher would become the new prime minister.

Australia promised to provide an expeditionary force of 20,000 men, which became known as the Australian Imperial Force (AIF). This force was to be made up of volunteers for overseas posting because under Australian legislation compulsory service did not allow for engagement beyond Australian shores. When enlistment began on 8 August recruiting stations were beset by volunteers. Thousands of young Australians from all parts of the continent left behind their jobs, farms, businesses, communities and their loved ones to sign up for active duty. On 1 November a great convoy of transports carrying both Australian and New Zealand troops steamed off for Europe. Most of them had little military training.

But the ships were diverted to Egypt instead, because not long after the troops had set sail for the European front, Turkey had entered the war on Germany's side. The German–Turkish alliance would effectively prevent Russia from being defended by the allies.

In Egypt, apart from undergoing further training, the troops were organised into an army corps of three divisions – the 1st Australian Division, a New Zealand and Australian division, and a mounted division made up of the 1st Australian Light Horse Brigade and the New Zealand Mounted Rifles. The army corps was named the Australian and New Zealand Army Corps. The initials of which formed the word ANZAC, a word that would live from then on in the annals of Australian history.

Then came a very ambitious plan. By January 1915 Russia needed to relieve its troops in the Caucasus where Turkish troops had mounted an aggressive assault. Russia appealed to Britain to undertake a diversionary operation to draw Turkish troops from the Eastern Front. Winston Churchill, then First Lord of the Admiralty, thought up a more courageous plan than a diversionary attack. He proposed a naval attack of the Dardenelles and pushing through to Constantinople, thereby knocking Turkey out of the war, increasing support for the allies, and allowing sea communication with Russia.

But when it became clear that naval action alone would not be successful, the original plan evolved into deploying the Anzacs to seize Gallipoli. At midnight on Sunday 25 April, Allied troopships lay waiting on a calm Aegean sea, under what Charles Bean, Australia's official war correspondent, described as 'a perfect moonlit night'. The Australian troops, especially those selected to go ashore first, were supposed to be catching up on sleep. Instead they were on deck keyed up for what was ahead. Some told yarns or sang songs, some wrote letters home, their words often full of cheer and assurances of returning home safely, while others nervously smoked cigarettes, their faces a mix of fear and hope. Perhaps all were keenly aware that this was an historic moment, but as they readied themselves for the assault, none would have guessed that Gallipoli would become hallowed legend.

The campaign to seize the peninsula at Gallipoli lasted nine months. It was never accomplished. When the Anzac force was evacuated, of the approximately 45,000 Australians who passed through Gallipoli, 19,000 were wounded and almost 8,500 made the supreme sacrifice. The body of only one of the dead, Brigadier General William Bridges, was returned to Australia.

On 25 April of each year Australia celebrates Anzac Day, a national holiday commemorating the 1915 landing of the troops on Gallipoli. For many outsiders – that is to say, for the people of

Members of the Australian 45th Battalion in the advance trenches at Garter Point, in the Ypres Sector, Western Front, Belgium. (Photo 29 September 1917)

*The images on these pages are stills from the 2005 Australian film **Gallipoli** by award-winning Turkish director Tolga Örnek, narrated by Jeremy Irons and Sam Neill. Australian military historian Brad Manera, an expert on costumes and weapons, travelled to Turkey to check the historical accuracy in every scene.*

War I could certainly boast a fair share of victories. After the withdrawal from Gallipoli, Australians fighting on the Western Front in France against the Germans distinguished themselves with the capture of Messines Ridge in June 1917; their courage also shone through in the third battle of Ypres in November of that same year; they shared in the defence of Amiens and the defeat of the Germans at Villers-Bretonneux during March and April 1918; and then, on 8 August, at the third battle of the Somme, and aware that victory was nigh, each day the Australians were instrumental in gaining more and more ground from German defences and keeping them in retreat.

There are events more worthy of celebration than Gallipoli, not only in World War I, but also in many other conflicts around the globe since. Is Anzac Day a day of remembrance, reserved solely to mourn and honour the fallen? If this is so, then as author Les Carlyon has asked, why not remember 19 July 1916 when in only one night at Fromelles, in French Flanders, Australia lost 5,533 men? This figure is more than double the number killed on the morning of 25 April 1915.

Another significant sacrifice was at the battle at Pozières in the Somme, which began on 23 July 1916 and raged for more than six weeks. A mere 600 acres of French soil was reclaimed from the enemy, yet three Australian divisions suffered the loss of 23,000 men. As Charles

nations that had no direct engagement in this particular episode of the Great War – Anzac Day could present itself as a paradox. Why commemorate a campaign that ultimately failed? Why celebrate the anniversary of the day on which more than 2,000 Australian men in their prime were cut down by enemy fire?

Despite – or perhaps in spite of – the agony of defeat endured at Gallipoli, the efforts of Australian servicemen for the remainder of World

Bean wrote, Pozières 'was more densely sown with Australian sacrifice than any other place on earth'. To this day the proportion of ground gained compared to lives lost is incomprehensible, especially when one discovers that the British and French casualties at Pozières ran into the hundreds of thousands.

One need not look too far back in Australia's history to understand the significance of Gallipoli and to fathom why this tragic event is so deeply embedded in our nation's collective consciousness.

When World War I broke out on 4 August 1914, Australia was an ancient land, but a very young nation. Australians had previously fought other wars in the service of the mother country – notably in the Boer War in South Africa and the Boxer Rebellion in China, which by 1914 were still in living memory of most Australians. But the Great War of 1914–18 was the first in which Australians fought as citizens of the Commonwealth of Australia rather than as 'colonials'.

The first day of the twentieth century, 1 January 1901, marked the birth date of a new nation. When Britain's call to arms came on 4 August 1914, the Commonwealth of Australia was a mere thirteen years old – and those who answered the call were not much older. The required age for enlistment was twenty-one. Volunteers could sign up at eighteen, but before they could be accepted they needed written consent from a parent or guardian. Many under

*This scene from the film **Gallipoli** recreates the Australians overtaking the Turkish trenches at Lone Pine during the August offensive, 1915.*

the age limit falsified their years or forged a parent's signature; others simply pestered, cajoled or threatened their parents into giving consent. And parents did indeed give in, because, like most other Australians, they believed the war would be over in a few months and were motivated by loyalty to the mother country.

War is always fought on two levels. There is obviously the battle with arms, and then there is the battle of nerves. It is hard to imagine the emotional turmoil all families must have endured while waiting for news. When letters from their sons stopped arriving, mothers especially would have secretly feared the worst.

Tobruk, Libya 1941. Two soldiers of the 9th Australian Division light cigarettes from a home-made lighter consisting of a piece of metal for flint and a string for wick.

Castle, a hospital ship anchored a kilometre or so off Anzac Cove. He did not die from wounds inflicted by enemy fire, but from heart failure due to typhoid. His official papers claimed him to be eighteen years old. Only his mate, Cecil Hogan, had guessed he was younger; that was because Cecil too had lied about his age. He had put Jim at sixteen, like himself. But when Jim died he was actually just fourteen years and nine months old. Born on 3 January 1901, Jim was younger than the Commonwealth of Australia by two days, and is known as the youngest Anzac to have died at war.

It is not difficult to picture that mournful day in November. Amelia Martin might have been in kitchen, perhaps baking a birthday cake, when she heard the doorbell ring. She opened the door to the postman with the military letter in his hand. She didn't need to open it, for she knew instantly what it contained. She closed the door and started back for the kitchen knowing that life would never be the same again.

Jim was buried at sea, and like all other mothers who lost their sons, Amelia was deprived of a funeral and a grave to visit. The years that followed seemed empty, but full of the guilt of having signed Jim's letter of consent.

Remembrance of the Anzac landing at Gallipoli evokes thoughts about the willingness of Australians to sacrifice their lives for others. It is a willingness that remains undaunted time

On 13 November 1915 Amelia Martin was preparing celebrations for her daughter Annie's tenth birthday when she received a military letter. She opened it and read with horror that Private James Martin – her son Jim – had died at Gallipoli three weeks earlier.

Precisely seven months after the first landing, 25 October, Jim Martin died on the *Glenart*

after time – at the defence of Tobruk and on the Kokoda Track during World War II, the conflicts in Korea, Vietnam and the Middle East, and peace-keeping missions around the world.

But marking the Gallipoli legend is about more than sacrifice, it is also about the child orphaned, the wife widowed and the mother robbed of a child. It is rather ironic that the man who recognised this most keenly was Mustafa Kemal Atatürk, who was responsible for successfully countering the Australian advance up the main ridge of the peninsula on 25 April 1915. In 1934, as President of Turkey, Atatürk erected a monument at Anzac Cove on which were inscribed these words:

Those heroes that shed their blood
and lost their lives …
You are now lying in the soil of a friendly country.
Therefore rest in peace.
There is no difference between the Johnnies
and the Mehmets to us where they lie side by side
here in this country of ours …
You, the mothers
who sent their sons from faraway countries
wipe away your tears;
your sons are now lying in our bosom
and are in peace.
After having lost their lives on this land they have
become ours sons as well.

Commemorating the fallen at the Shrine of Remembrance, Melbourne, at the first Anzac Day Service after World War II, 25 April 1946.

Composer's Notes: Movement V *Immigration Scherzo*

A celebration of Australia's unique cultural identity.

The Australian National Anthem, 'Advance Australia Fair' by Peter McCormick, Scottish immigrant, schoolteacher and songwriter, is used as a musical template to embrace the music and sounds of the many nationalities of the world that make up our nation.

Music can be an exciting analogy for the potential of human beings to interact with each other once their inhibitions are gone: musical diversity is as beautiful as its social counterpart, the success of which is enjoyed in Australian society today. By continuing to build together, with good humour and sincere effort, we will all share an exciting, colourful future.

MOVEMENT V

Immigration Scherzo

Australia – stillborn forsaken land,
Surviving bare and tough as by surprise,
On the world's map a dish full of barren sand,
Yet full of life, sun-soaked birds' paradise.
For this dear land it's dawn, it's spring.
New-born, new-comer: 'Welcome! Needed here!'
To this new land young hearts will cling,
Each with a stormy past, from now on clear.
For us, who landed here by choice or luck,
Despite the fact that homelands can't move on,
Remains this land, a challenge to live on.
If this dries dead, our life's endeavour's stuck.

From 'Adopted Country' by Ivan Kobal, Slovenian labourer,
Snowy Mountains Scheme (translated from Slovene)

*British children aboard the **Fairsea**, eager for a look at their new home, 1956. The liner brought 1,470 migrants on the voyage from the United Kingdom. Among these there were more than 530 children under the age of 14 years.*

Something miraculous happened in Australia on 7 August 1946. A twelve-year-old Indonesian boy by the name of Bas Wie arrived at Darwin airport from Timor. Well, that's hardly remarkable, let alone miraculous. Though how he arrived is.

At Kupang, in Timor, Bas Wie had hoisted himself up into one of the wheel bays of a Dutch Air Force DC3 that was headed for Australia. When discovered by the ground crew at Darwin, he was unconscious, his body covered in burns. His clothes were soaked in his own blood and he was suffering from hypothermia. It was a miracle he was alive, a miracle that once in flight he wasn't crushed by the wheel when it retracted into the bay, or hadn't died from the lack of oxygen, or been burnt to death by the terrible heat from the aircraft's engine. It was an even greater miracle that he hadn't fallen to his death when, at 500 metres above the earth, the wheels dropped into position for landing.

At Royal Darwin Hospital the next day Bas Wie revealed what everyone had already suspected. He was a stowaway, an orphan running from misery and abuse at a time when Australia had been expelling Indonesians seeking refuge because of the war. The only other thing Bas divulged when interviewed by immigration officials was his wish to stay in Australia.

A few days later the Department of Immigration announced it would deport Bas as soon as he was well enough to travel. Public outrage was immediate and the story made world headlines. For three months Bas lay recuperating in a hospital bed, and public pressure steadily increased until Australia's first Minister for Immigration, Arthur Calwell, finally caved in. It was a long battle thereafter, for although Bas was allowed to stay, it took ten years before he was allowed to be adopted or become an Australian citizen.

Australia was once far from being a place that people from diverse cultures could call home. The White Australia Policy was based on a rigid belief in white supremacy and a fear of non-European races. The Immigration Restriction Bill 1901, based on similar legislation in South Africa, was introduced at the first session of the new nation's parliament. When Alfred Deakin, known as the 'Father of Federation', detailed the main points of the Bill, he knew it would not be hotly debated. At the conclusion of his speech, Deakin said: 'Members on both sides of the House, and of all sections of all parties – those in office and those out of office – with the people behind them,

TOP LEFT: *Bas Wie holding a model sailing ship that he made for the Driver family, who looked after him at Government House in Darwin.*

BOTTOM LEFT: *Australia welcomed millions of migrants after World War II.*

are all united in the unalterable resolve that the Commonwealth of Australia shall mean a "white Australia", and that from now henceforth all alien elements within it shall be diminished.'

From early settlement immigration contributed to population numbers for reasons of opportunity as well as escape. Many Australian families are descended from generations of early migrants, including thousands of fortune hunters from Europe and China in particular attracted to the gold rush, those forced to seek new opportunities after economic trouble in their home countries, and those in fear of persecution. However, up to World War II, Australia was still considered by many as a part of Britain, and Empire Day was still celebrated each year.

The story of Bas Wie's flight over the Timor Sea, less than a year after the end of World War II, coincided with the beginning of the end for the White Australia policy. A testimony of the extraordinary risks some people will take to come to Australia, Bas Wie's acceptance could also be seen as a first step in the creation of a uniquely Australian multicultural society.

The government that had tried to deport Bas Wie also implemented programs that resulted in the biggest wave of migrant intake in Australia's entire history. Before World War II the make-up of Australia's population was predominantly British, but immediately after the war no other country

Mixed emotions are displayed on the faces of migrants arriving in Australia 1966. (David Moore, 1927–2003)

in the world accepted as many non-British immigrants as Australia. An assisted migrant scheme negotiated with Britain was first extended to ex-service personnel from the United States, then soon after to ex-servicemen from the Netherlands, Norway, France, Belgium and Denmark.

After the war, Australia desperately needed to boost its population. Settlement had begun less than 200 years earlier and there was still a lot of work to be done. In short, Australia needed people to do it. The nation was rich in untapped natural resources but a shortage in labour was holding back the country's development. A change in the population mix was inevitable when on 7 July 1949 an Act of the Commonwealth Parliament established the Snowy Mountains Hydro-Electric Scheme. The scheme was the most ambitious engineering project ever undertaken in Australia, and consisted of seven power stations, sixteen major dams, 145 kilometres of tunnels and 80 kilometres of aqueducts. It took twenty-five years to complete.

Not only was the Snowy Mountains Scheme a great accomplishment of engineering, but it was also a supreme achievement in building a diverse Australian society. It would not have begun, let alone been envisaged, if Australia could not have welcomed huge numbers of immigrants. It is widely regarded as the birthplace of multiculturalism. While the existing Australians formed the largest single national group, more than two-

In one of history's great migrations, more than six million people have crossed the world to settle in Australia.

thirds of all workers were new arrivals, escaping or lured away from the war-scarred lands of Europe. In the twenty-five years it took for the scheme to be completed, more than 100,000 people were employed to work on its construction, and of that figure almost 70,000 of them came from thirty-one different countries.

Even back in 1949, the Snowy Mountains Scheme was regarded as ambitious, and its name reverberates through the years as an amazing social achievement. Alliances were formed between people who, a mere four years earlier, had exchanged bullets. There is one renowned Snowy Mountains' story concerning a couple of former enemies watching a Hollywood recreation of the battle at Dunkirk. During interval, a worker with a German accent piped up and declared that the film was a 'load of rubbish'. Somewhere

Paticipants in Turkish national costume perform traditional Turkish dances in Australia Day celebrations in Melbourne.

Naturalisation of migrants, part of Australia Day activities at Circular Quay, Sydney, 1991

nearby another worker responded in an unmistakeable Cockney voice, 'How the hell would you know?' As the two squared off, the men soon came realise that they were both at Dunkirk: one was fighting from the air while another was fighting back from the water. Instead of opening up past wounds, a lifelong friendship ensued between the pair as they talked of their respective experiences.

The Scheme also made for some very amusing stories. One is of a European migrant who worked as an ambulance driver. He seemed, however, to display medical skills and knowledge beyond those required of an ambulance driver. Apparently on one occasion, this ambulance driver had the gall to interrupt a tracheotomy as the surgeon was about to make an incision. 'Stop!' shouted the driver, 'that's not right.' The surgeon was shocked by the interruption, but had the good sense to pause and reach for a medical reference book so that he could explain that he was following the correct procedure. The ambulance driver replied, 'Well, that was correct when I wrote it, but things have changed since then.'

In August 1973, as the Snowy Mountains Scheme neared completion, the word 'multicul-

The Welcome Wall, 100 metres long beside the Australian National Maritime Musuem in Sydney's Darling Harbour, commemorates the millions of 'first families' who have arrived at this country's shores.

tural' was used for the first time in an official government paper. However, the adoption of multiculturalism did not cause an immediate surge in migrant numbers. This was largely because under pressure of a weak economy, the government was forced to reduce the yearly migration quota.

After the dismissal of the Labor government in 1975, the Liberal government supported the shift to multiculturalism. Overseas conflicts had further profound impacts on shaping the face of Australian society. The Vietnam War had ended in 1975 and the first wave of Vietnamese 'boat people' arrived in April 1976. By January 1983 Australia had accepted almost 70,000 Indochinese arrivals. Then in late 1975, the outbreak of civil war in Lebanon ushered in another wave of refugees. Entry restictions were eased, allowing Lebanese people already settled in Australia to sponsor family members. By 1981, approximately 16,000 Lebanese had migrated to Australia. There was an increase in immigration from a diverse range of countries. In less than five years multiculturalism became a substantive feature of Australia life.

Most of Australia's migrant population after World War II had come from poverty and famine, social injustice and political persecution, or from homelands ravaged by war. Referred to at the time as 'New Australians', some had come to live free and to live among equals; others came for refuge; most came to work and improve their lives. Most came to Australia to escape something, but not to forget their culture or beliefs. They could do so if they wished, but they were proud of their heritage. Australia fostered that pride and in the process the nation was enriched.

Australia's population today is made up of people from over 200 countries. There are just as many languages spoken, and about 100 religious denominations are represented. Students and professional people from around the world are advancing their careers and providing the skills necessary for Australia's prosperity. And refugees from places of poverty, conflict and persecution are today still beginning new lives in a welcoming society built from those who came before them.

By the way, Bas Wie went on to enjoy a long career with the public service and started new generations, with five Australian children and seven grandchildren.

Australia has become a country that lets its people be proud of their heritage. Every day in every corner of Australia there is abundant evidence of the contribution of migrants in all fields of life – art, food, fashion, architecture, language, music, design, commerce, medicine, politics, science, welfare, religion and education. Every day is a celebration of that legacy. Having come from all corners of the globe, migrants have shaped Australia into a great mosaic of living cultures.

Composer's Notes: MOVEMENT VI *My Country Australia*

What it means to be Australian – inspired by the words of Dorothea Mackellar.

The prelude of this final movement depicts the rising of the sun on a new day – the first day of our future. The themes of 'My Country Australia' are developed on clarinets and horns in fragments and previous movements of the symphony are revisited. We hear the Rainbow Serpent, the theme of 'The Ships', the mother's lament from the 'Pie Jesu', and the theme of 'The Red Centre'.

The whirl of themes and ideas stops dead in its tracks as a solo didgeridoo enters. The sounds of the southern lights are heard as the excitement builds to the entry of the choir and soloist and the climax of the Symphony of Australia.

In the history of Australian literature and the hearts of Australians, the stirring poem 'My Country' by Dorothea Mackellar has a special place. The Symphony of Australia comes to its grand conclusion with the words of the poem, as the soloist begins: 'I love a sunburnt country, a land of sweeping plains ...'

MOVEMENT VI

My Country Australia

I love a sunburnt country,
A land of sweeping plains,
Of ragged mountain ranges,
Of droughts and flooding rains.
I love her far horizons
I love her jewel-sea,
Her beauty and her terror –
The wide brown land for me!

Dorothea Mackellar 'My Country'

Whether you were born here or you have come from elsewhere, the Australian experience invariably includes falling in love with this vast country. For the most part Australia is a naked land, its interior quite deserted of people, yet it wields a magnetism which, like the moon upon the tides, tugs at the heart and stimulates endless praise in the minds of many. This allure is not a new thing. It can be traced back to the days even before British settlement, to those first audacious explorers of the fifteenth century – the Spaniards, Dutch and Portuguese – who travelled far across uncharted waters in search of the Great Southern Land. What is the magnetic power of this country?

Among the first to pinpoint this country's charm was Dorothea Mackellar, the author of the iconic poem 'My Country', considered by many to have literally captured the sublime and unceasing connection of Australians to the land.

Mackellar began writing 'My Country' in 1904 while on a visit to England. She rewrote the poem several times after returning to Australia. Four years later, finally satisfied with it, she sent the poem to the London *Spectator* and on 5 September 1908 it was published under her original title of 'Core of My Heart'. It was later retitled 'My Country' and included in Mackellar's first book of poetry *The Closed Door and Other Verses*, which was published in Melbourne in 1911.

For too long it has been wrongly assumed that Dorothea Mackellar wrote her most celebrated poem while in England, homesick for Australia. Nothing could be further from the truth. Mackellar enjoyed travelling overseas, which she did quite extensively, and England was one of the destinations she favoured the most. She was certainly not made to feel unwelcome there, nor did she lack companionship. Her numerous friends were of considerable influence and high social rank – politicians, academics, bankers, artists and fellow travellers in the world of letters – and as a member of the moneyed elite, her time there was filled with a round of vibrant social engagements at dinner, the theatre, museums, and concerts. Joseph Conrad, one of England's most renowned novelists, counted as one of her closest friends.

The love of field and coppice
Of green and shaded lanes
Of ordered woods and gardens
Is running in your veins –
Strong love of grey-blue distance
Brown streams and soft dim skies
I know but cannot share it,
My love is otherwise.

The first verse, which is an acknowledgement of England's mannered beauty, is a part of the poem that is rarely brought to mind. At times, it has been deliberately omitted by particular publishers. The English countryside as evoked by Mackellar is

neither depressive nor oppressive, and clearly the words are not those of a homesick young lady. She has instead lauded the English countryside, inspired by her memorable visits there.

It was not homesickness but annoyance that led Mackellar to put pen to paper. She was irritated by the attitudes of the women of her social class who sought to erase or at least deny Australia as the country of their birth. Even though most were fourth-generation Australians, this was an early form of the 'cultural cringe', in which they attributed their wealth and social standing to England rather than the opportunities given to them by Australia. She was especially annoyed whenever leaving for England and her friends would say how lucky she was to be going 'back home', or would intimate that the heads of Sydney Harbour were like prison gates closing behind her.

But it was Australia and particularly the Australian landscape that exerted an influence on Dorothea Mackellar rather than her class or social position. The second verse is one of the best known verses of Australian poetry.

I love a sunburnt country,
A land of sweeping plains,
Of ragged mountain ranges,
Of droughts and flooding rains.
I love her far horizons
I love her jewel-sea,
Her beauty and her terror –
The wide brown land for me!

Dorothea Mackellar was born on 1 July 1885 at Dunara, her family's home on Point Piper, a five-acre property with a view of the city on one side and of Rose Bay on the other. She was one of four children, the only daughter of Sir Charles Kinnaird Mackellar, a renowned physician and parliamentarian. From an early age she received private lessons in painting, fencing and languages – French, Italian, German and Spanish – all of which she spoke fluently. Hers was a comfortable and privileged life, and she enjoyed all the benefits the city could offer.

But Dorothea was also drawn to and deeply enchanted by the country. It was at the family's first country property Torryburn, near East Gresford, not far from Maitland in New South Wales, where she lived an Alice-in-Wonderland existence and first experienced the extremes of the Australian outback.

The stark white ring-barked forests
All tragic to the moon
The sapphire-misted mountains
The hot gold hush of noon –
Green tangle of the brushes
Where the lithe lianas coil
And orchids deck the tree-tops,
And ferns the warm dark soil.

The Mackellar family bought a number of other properties over the years, including two in the Gunnedah district – Kurrumbede and The

Rampadells. Dorothea called them home as much as she did Dunara. She saw the land in drought, in flood, and ravaged by fire, and she saw it green and lush and teeming with wildlife. By the time she came to write 'My Country' she had realised that both the 'beauty' and 'terror' of the land were all of one piece.

The Australian landscape gave Dorothea maturity and knowledge beyond her years, and an overwhelming sense of freedom from all forms of restrictions, especially class. She had little time for people who valued comfort above beauty. She understood how they felt because their backgrounds had given them no reason to feel otherwise, but she was glad she could appreciate the day-to-day beauty of nature's life and death struggle.

> Core of my heart, my country!
> Her pitiless blue sky,
> When sick at heart, around us
> We see the cattle die –
> And then the grey clouds gather,
> And we can bless again
> The drumming of an army,
> The steady, soaking rain.

In Australia no matter how tough life can be, there is always the belief that the 'drought' will break. No wonder her poem was a favourite among Australian troops during World War I. For Mackellar Australia was a land offering great opportunity, but opportunity not handed over on

A scene of striking Australian outback colours west of Broken Hill, New South Wales.

a silver platter. This is why she detested the fashion among her peers to give all credit to England. The elements test Australians, and if they pass the test the land might give more than they could have ever hoped for. Many people have come to Australia and they have come with nothing, yet they have succeeded in turning nothing into something. In Australia one realises that you can make your destiny.

Dorothea Mackellar was both poet and prophet. Her sense of freedom was one that could only develop with a unique perception of the Australian landscape. 'My Country' stands as a constant reminder of the qualities that have made this country great. Her words will echo through the ages and continue to find resonance in all aspects of Australian life.

From its ancient beginnings Australia has always been a land of dreaming. In such a rich and diverse landscape, in such an exciting and varied culture, dreaming comes naturally. As all Australians contemplate the future of our nation

A handful of Victoria's remaining 'twelve' apostles, off the south coast of Australia. The ocean continues to erode and demolish these unique remnants of the land.

we should encourage one another, and our neighbours, to put those dreams into action with all the dogged determination that the Aussie can muster. By continuing to rise together to build our future on common goals, we, as Australians, will continue to turn our dreams into stunning reality, defined by our love for our country, our people and our ideals.

Australians, wherever they are in the world, feel the pull of their homeland. To some, Australia is a harsh and strange place to build a life, but to the Aussie it is a paradise on earth, a jewel of the southern seas: a place that is home.

An opal-hearted country,
A wilful, lavish land –
All you who have not loved her,
You will not understand –
Though earth holds many splendours,
Wherever I may die,
I know to what brown country
My homing thoughts will fly.

The world-renowned natural icon of Australia, Uluru, also known as Ayers Rock. This huge sandstone monolith, set in a contrasting sand plain environment, stuns visitors with its many changes in appearance, especially its red glow at twilight.

Acknowledgements

Symphony of Australia Music and lyrics by Gavin Lockley

THE MUSIC

Sydney Symphony

Brett Weymark — *Conductor*
Kirsten Williams — *Concertmaster*

Cantillation

Philip Chu — *Chorusmaster*

INTRODUCTION
Jon English *speaker*
Gavin Lockley *piano*

I DREAMTIME
Matthew Doyle *didgeridoo*
Harry Adkins *treble soprano*
Janet Webb *flute*
Shefali Pryor *oboe*

II THE SHIPS
Jon English *singer and speaker*
The Sydney Tribe (Matthew Doyle, Glen Doyle, Clarence Slockee, Jacquelyn Davison) *singers and percussionists*

III THE RED CENTRE
Rick Miller, Brian Nixon *timpani*
Sharolyn Kimmorley *piano*

IV PIE JESU
Renae Martin *mezzo-soprano*

V IMMIGRATION SCHERZO
Heather Lee *singer*
Kim Cunio *s'tar*
Riley Lee *shakuhachi*
Sarangan Sriranganathan *sitar*
Tom (Anthony) Ferris *acoustic guitar*
Fernando Arancibia *pan pipes*

VI MY COUNTRY AUSTRALIA
Damian Humbley *tenor*
Matthew Doyle *didgeridoo*
Leon Gaer *electric bass, fretless electric bass*
Pete Skelton *drums*

Recorded and mastered at Trackdown Scoring Stage, Sydney
Sharolyn Kimmorley — Recording producer
Simon Leadley — Recording and mixing engineer
Daniel Brown — Mastering engineer, recording and mixing engineer, Movement I
Torei Lista — Music editor
Adam Vanryne — Additional recording, production, remixing and mastering
Jay Collie — Sequencer
Sofie Loizou — Technical consultant

THE STORY

Simon Best — Project manager
Raffaele Caputo — Writer
Bob Andersen — Consultant
Lauren Statham — Designer
Lisa Barker — Researcher
Neil Conning — Editor

With special thanks to the Estate of the Late Dorothea Mackellar for words from 'My Country' by Dorothea Mackellar originally published as 'Core of my Heart' (Movement VI); Wendy Pye; Catherine Lockley for additional choral lyrics; Victor Steffensen of the Traditional Knowledge Recording Project, Cape York; Keith Rossi of the Returned and Services League; Kenneth Youdale DFC; and Clyde Thompson and members of the Royal Flying Doctor Service.

Picture credits

Lauren Statham, Alice Graphics (p. 26); M.J.M Carter AO Collection 1993, Art Gallery of South Australia, Adelaide (p. 27); Australian National Maritime Museum (p. 16, 47); Australian War Memorial (pp. 33–5, 38); Donated to the Australian War Memorial by Mrs L.J. McNicol (p. 32); M.V. Gulliver, Melbourne, Australian War Memorial (p. 39); Dreamstime.com (p. 25, 50); Dreamstime.com © Linda & Colin Mckie (p. 50); Dreamstime.com © Graham Prentice; Getty Images (p. 45); istockphoto (pp. 48, 51–2, 55); istockphoto, Timothy Ball (p. 24); Lonely Planet Images, © Mitch Reardon (p. 31); Natural Wanders © Steven David Miller (p. 8); David Moore, 1966. © L., M., K. and M. Moore (p. 44); Dorothy Fisher Davidson, Museum Victoria. (p. 43); National Library of Australia (pp. 17–20, 29–30); National Library of Australia, Rex Nan Kivell Collection (p. 22); National Archives of Australia (pp. 12, 41–2, 46); Northern Territory Library, Roderick Collection (p. 42); Photolibrary (pp. 9, 11, 14–15, 40); Photolibrary/ Radius Images/Jupiter Images (front cover, p. 2); © Jan Rihak (p. 13); Courtesy of Tolga Örnek, Ronin Films, Canberra Australia (pp. 36–7); Courtesy of the Royal Flying Doctor Service (SE Division) (p. 53); Courtesy Ian Sanderson (p. 10); State Library of New South Wales (p. 21); State Library of Tasmania, W.L. Crowther Library (p. 28); Stockexchange (p. 54); Stockexpert (p. 49)
Picture research and permissions: Kate Chisholm and Lee Floyd, Upstream Productions

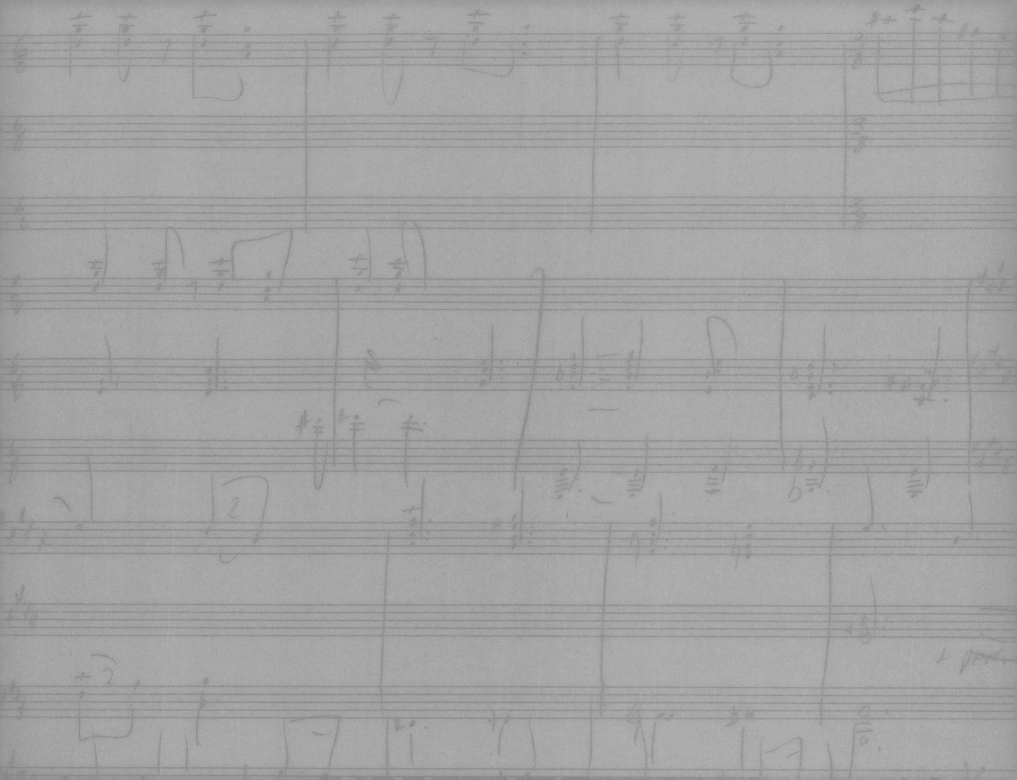